MathFlare

Name: ______________________

Class: __________

Teacher: ______________________

Introduction

As parents and educators, we recognize the pivotal role mathematics plays in shaping a child's academic journey and future success. Yet, the path to mathematical proficiency can often seem daunting, fraught with challenges and complexities. That's where the transformative power of MathFlare Workbooks shine through, illuminating the way forward with clarity, precision, and purpose.

Introducing MathFlare Workbooks – a beacon of guidance, a testament to excellence, and a catalyst for achievement. Crafted with meticulous care and expertise, MathFlare Workbooks stand as paragons of educational excellence, designed to nurture young minds, ignite a passion for learning, and develop a deep-rooted understanding of mathematical concepts.

Picture this: your child eagerly delves into the pages of Mathflare Workbook, greeted by a step-by-step guide illuminated with vivid examples that demystify complex mathematical concepts. With each turn of the page, they embark on a journey of discovery, encountering thoughtfully curated practice questions that reinforce learning and hone problem-solving skills. And when they unveil the answers to those very questions, a sense of accomplishment blossoms within them – a tangible reward for their hard work and dedication.

But MathFlare Workbooks are more than just tools for learning; they are pathways to comprehension, fostering a deep-seated understanding of mathematical concepts through a sequential, logical flow. From fundamental principles to advanced problem-solving strategies, every chapter builds upon the last, ensuring a robust foundation upon which future knowledge can be constructed.

As parents, we yearn for nothing more than to see our children thrive, to witness the spark of inspiration ignited within them as they conquer academic challenges with confidence and poise. MathFlare Workbooks serve as partners in this noble endeavor, offering not just practice questions, but the keys to unlocking a world of opportunity.

And for teachers, MathFlare Workbooks stand as invaluable allies in the quest to cultivate mathematical proficiency in the classroom. With answers readily available, instructors can focus on guiding and nurturing their students, confident in the knowledge that MathFlare Workbooks provide a solid framework upon which to build.

In the pages of MathFlare Workbooks, we find not just the promise of academic excellence, but the seeds of a brighter tomorrow. So let us embrace the power of mathematics, let us champion the journey of learning, and let us pave the way for a generation of young minds poised to shape the world. With MathFlare Workbooks as our guide, the possibilities are infinite, and the future, bright.

Table of Contents

MathFlare
MATH WORKBOOK
Grade 2
Step by Step Guide and Essential Practice with Answers
Addition Subtraction
Multiplication
Place Value and Expanded Notations
Geometry
MathFlare Publishing

MathFlare
MATH WORKBOOK
Grade 2-3
Step by Step Guide and Essential Practice with Answers
Addition Subtraction
Multiplication and Division
Place Value and Expanded Notations
Geometry
MathFlare Publishing

MathFlare
MATH WORKBOOK
Grade 3
Step by Step Guide and Essential Practice with Answers
Multiplication and Division
Decimals
Place Value and Expanded Notations
Fractions and Geometry
MathFlare Publishing

MathFlare
MATH WORKBOOK
Grade 1
Step by Step Guide and Essential Practice with Answers
Counting and Numbers
Addition and Subtraction
Place Value and Expanded Notations
Understanding Time
MathFlare Publishing

MathFlare
MATH WORKBOOK
Grade 1-2
Step by Step Guide and Essential Practice with Answers
Counting and Numbers
Addition and Subtraction
Place Value and Expanded Notations
Understanding Time
MathFlare Publishing

MathFlare
MATH WORKBOOK
Grade 3-4
Step by Step Guide and Essential Practice with Answers
Addition Subtraction
Multiplication Division
Place Value and Expanded Notations
Fractions and Geometry
MathFlare Publishing

MathFlare
MATH WORKBOOK
Grade 4
Step by Step Guide and Essential Practice with Answers
Addition Subtraction
Multiplication Division
Place Value and Expanded Notations
Fractions and Geometry
MathFlare Publishing

MathFlare
MATH WORKBOOK
Grade 4-5
Step by Step Guide and Essential Practice with Answers
Multiplication Division
Place Value and Expanded Notations
Fractions and Geometry
Unit Conversion
MathFlare Publishing

MathFlare
MATH WORKBOOK
5
Step by Step Guide and Essential Practice with Answers
Multiplication Division
Place Value and Expanded Notations
Fractions and Geometry
Unit Conversion
MathFlare Publishing

MathFlare
MATH WORKBOOK
5-6
Step by Step Guide and Essential Practice with Answers
Multiplication Division
Place Value and Expanded Notations
Fractions and Geometry
Units and Statistics
MathFlare Publishing

MathFlare
MATH WORKBOOK
6
Step by Step Guide and Essential Practice with Answers
Integers and Statistics
Arithmetic and Pre-Algebra
Fractions and Geometry
Ratio and Percentage
MathFlare Publishing

MathFlare
MATH WORKBOOK
6-7
Step by Step Guide and Essential Practice with Answers
Arithmetic and Pre-Algebra
Ratio, Percent Proportion
Geometry
Statistics
MathFlare Publishing

MathFlare
MATH WORKBOOK
7
Step by Step Guide and Essential Practice with Answers
Pre-Algebra
Ratio, Percent Proportion
Geometry
Statistics
MathFlare Publishing

MathFlare
MATH WORKBOOK
7-8
Step by Step Guide and Essential Practice with Answers
Pre-Algebra
Ratio, Percent Proportion
Geometry and Cartesian Plane
Statistics
MathFlare Publishing

MathFlare
MATH WORKBOOK
8-9
Step by Step Guide and Essential Practice with Answers
Pre-Algebra
Ratio, Proportion and Percentage
Linear Equations
Geometry and Cartesian Plane
MathFlare Publishing

MathFlare
MATH WORKBOOK
8
Step by Step Guide and Essential Practice with Answers
Pre-Algebra
Percentage
Linear Equations
Geometry
MathFlare Publishing

Ratio and Proportion and Percentage

A proportional relationship between two quantities exists when they have a constant ratio or when one is a multiple of the other. In other words, if we increase one quantity, the other quantity will increase or decrease by the same factor. For example, if we double one quantity, the other quantity will also double.

Let's solve a problem:

$$\frac{}{9} = \frac{8}{18}$$

Step 1: Cross Multiply: Cross multiply by multiplying the numerator of one fraction by the denominator of the other, and vice versa:

$$x \times 18 = 9 \times 8$$

Step 2: Solve for the Unknown: Perform the multiplication on both sides of the equation:

$$18x = 72$$

Step 3: Divide Both Sides by the Coefficient of the Unknown: To isolate x, divide both sides of the equation by the coefficient of x, which is 18:

$$\frac{18x}{18} = \frac{72}{18}$$

$$x = 4$$

Step 4: Verify Check your solution by substituting x = 4 back into the original equation:

$$\frac{4}{9} = \frac{8}{18}$$

Since both sides are equal, the solution x = 4 is correct.

Ratio and Proportion Word Problems

We can use the concept of proportionality in solving many word problems, for example:

If a car travels 620 miles in six hours, how far can it travel in 12 hours?

Since the car travels a certain distance in a certain amount of time, we can assume that the distance traveled is directly proportional to the time taken.

Let d be the distance the car can travel in 12 hours.

We can set up a proportion:

$$\frac{\text{Distance1}}{\text{Time1}} = \frac{\text{Distance2}}{\text{Time2}}$$

Substituting the given values:

$$\frac{620 \text{ miles}}{6 \text{ hours}} = \frac{d}{12 \text{ hours}}$$

Now, let's solve for d.

$$d = \frac{620 \times 12}{6} = \frac{7440}{6} = 1240$$

So, the car can travel 1240 miles in 12 hours.

Percentage

Percentage is a way of expressing a number as a fraction of 100. It is commonly used to represent proportions, rates, and comparisons. The symbol "%" is used to denote percentages.

To calculate a percentage, we multiply the given number by the appropriate fraction or decimal equivalent.

How to calculate a percentage:

Convert Percentage to Decimal: If the percentage is given as a percentage value (e.g., 25%), convert it to its decimal equivalent by dividing by 100.

$$\text{For example, 25\% as a decimal is } \frac{25}{100} = 0.25$$

Multiply: Multiply the decimal equivalent of the percentage by the given number. This gives us the portion of the number that represents the percentage.

$$100 \times 0.25 = 25\%$$

Result: The result is the calculated percentage value.

For example, to calculate 25% of 80:

Convert 25% to a decimal: 25% = 0.25.

Multiply 0.25 by 80: $0.25 \times 80 = 20$. The result is 20.

Percent Word Problems

Percent word problems involve situations where percentages are used to calculate quantities or amounts. These problems often require converting percentages to decimals and then applying them to the given values.

For example:

Bella bought a pair of shoes for $90.00. If she paid an additional 90% for taxes, how much in total did she pay for the shoes?

- Bella bought a pair of shoes for $90.00.

- She paid an additional 90% for taxes.

Calculate 90% of $90:

Tax= 90% × 90

Tax= 0.90 × 90

Tax= $81

Add the tax amount to the original price:

Total cost= $90 + $81

Total cost= $171

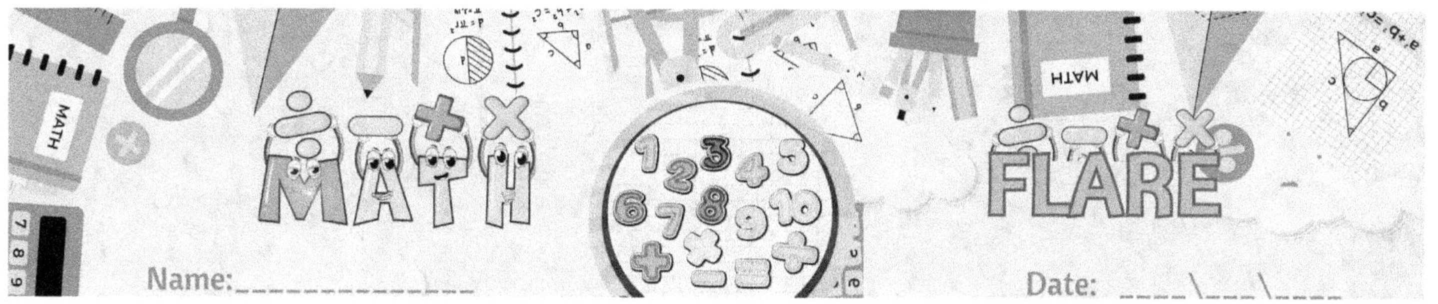

Proportional Relationship

1. $\dfrac{1}{} = \dfrac{6}{60}$

2. $\dfrac{9}{10} = \dfrac{18}{}$

3. $\dfrac{1}{} = \dfrac{10}{20}$

4. $\dfrac{3}{4} = \dfrac{24}{}$

5. $\dfrac{2}{3} = \dfrac{14}{}$

6. $\dfrac{2}{7} = \dfrac{}{56}$

7. $\dfrac{3}{5} = \dfrac{12}{}$

8. $\dfrac{}{11} = \dfrac{80}{110}$

9. $\dfrac{7}{8} = \dfrac{42}{}$

10. $\dfrac{}{6} = \dfrac{6}{36}$

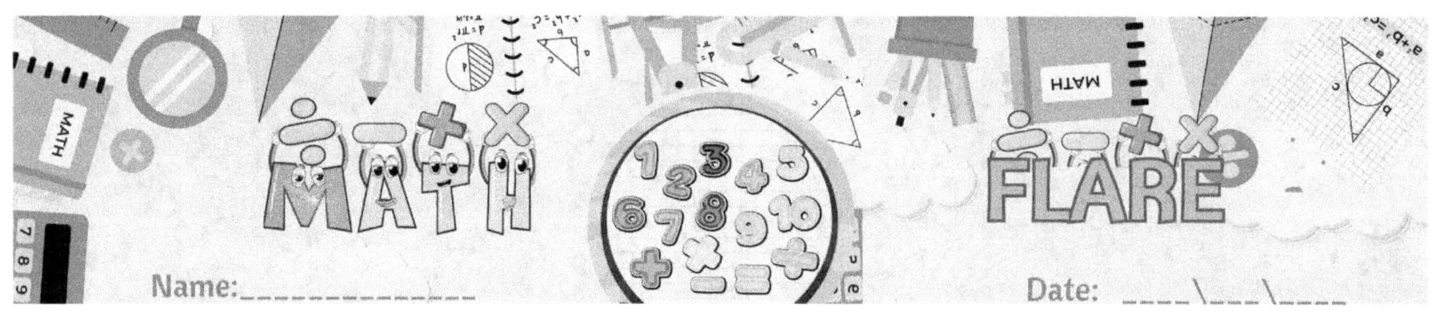

11. $\dfrac{3}{} = \dfrac{30}{90}$

12. $\dfrac{2}{12} = \dfrac{10}{}$

13. $\dfrac{5}{11} = \dfrac{25}{}$

14. $\dfrac{7}{10} = \dfrac{}{70}$

15. $\dfrac{9}{12} = \dfrac{}{60}$

16. $\dfrac{}{3} = \dfrac{8}{24}$

17. $\dfrac{6}{7} = \dfrac{}{21}$

18. $\dfrac{1}{8} = \dfrac{}{24}$

19. $\dfrac{1}{} = \dfrac{9}{45}$

20. $\dfrac{2}{} = \dfrac{16}{32}$

21. $\dfrac{3}{9} = \dfrac{6}{}$

22. $\dfrac{}{6} = \dfrac{24}{36}$

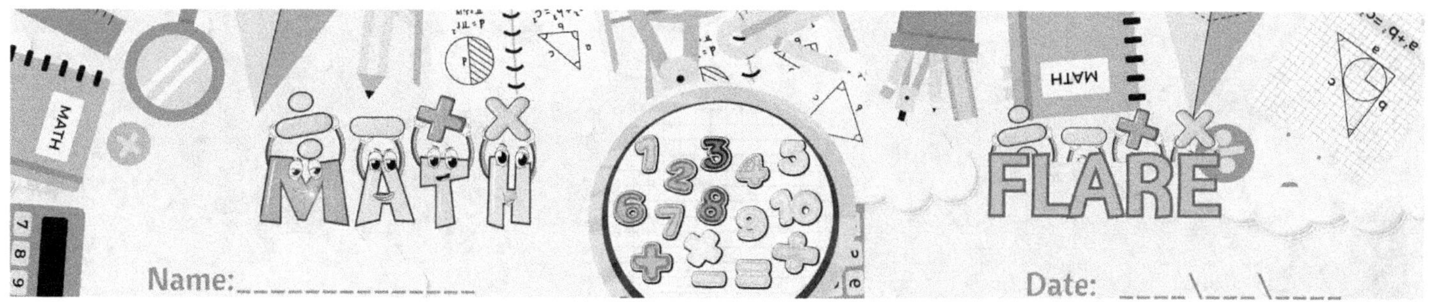

23. $\dfrac{1}{2} = \dfrac{5}{}$

24. $\dfrac{3}{} = \dfrac{12}{16}$

25. $\dfrac{10}{12} = \dfrac{}{120}$

26. $\dfrac{4}{6} = \dfrac{8}{}$

27. $\dfrac{}{7} = \dfrac{6}{21}$

28. $\dfrac{}{11} = \dfrac{42}{66}$

29. $\dfrac{2}{9} = \dfrac{}{72}$

30. $\dfrac{7}{} = \dfrac{49}{56}$

31. $\dfrac{}{2} = \dfrac{3}{6}$

32. $\dfrac{1}{} = \dfrac{7}{70}$

33. $\dfrac{1}{} = \dfrac{2}{6}$

34. $\dfrac{3}{5} = \dfrac{}{15}$

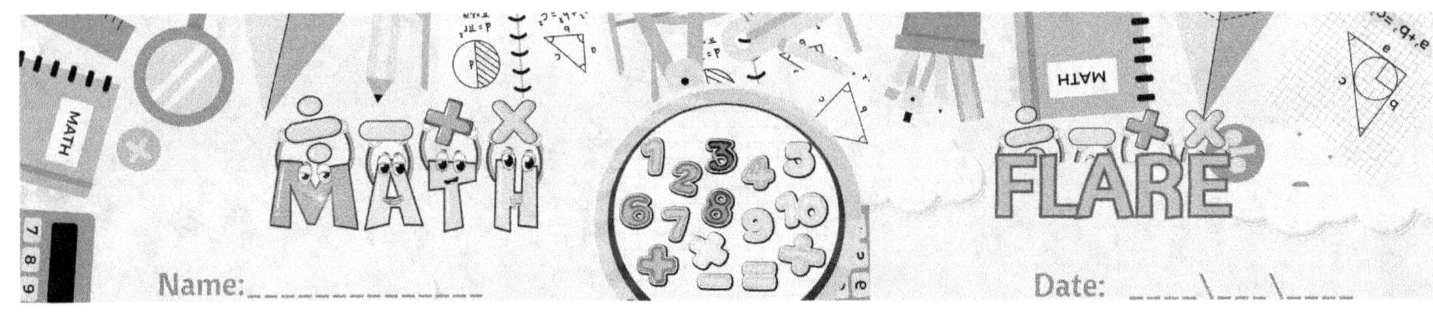

35. $\dfrac{1}{2} = \dfrac{}{12}$

36. $\dfrac{7}{} = \dfrac{35}{40}$

37. $\dfrac{2}{3} = \dfrac{}{9}$

38. $\dfrac{4}{12} = \dfrac{28}{}$

39. $\dfrac{}{10} = \dfrac{90}{100}$

40. $\dfrac{2}{5} = \dfrac{8}{}$

41. $\dfrac{1}{} = \dfrac{10}{90}$

42. $\dfrac{4}{6} = \dfrac{12}{}$

43. $\dfrac{7}{} = \dfrac{70}{110}$

44. $\dfrac{2}{8} = \dfrac{}{64}$

45. $\dfrac{6}{7} = \dfrac{60}{}$

46. $\dfrac{3}{5} = \dfrac{21}{}$

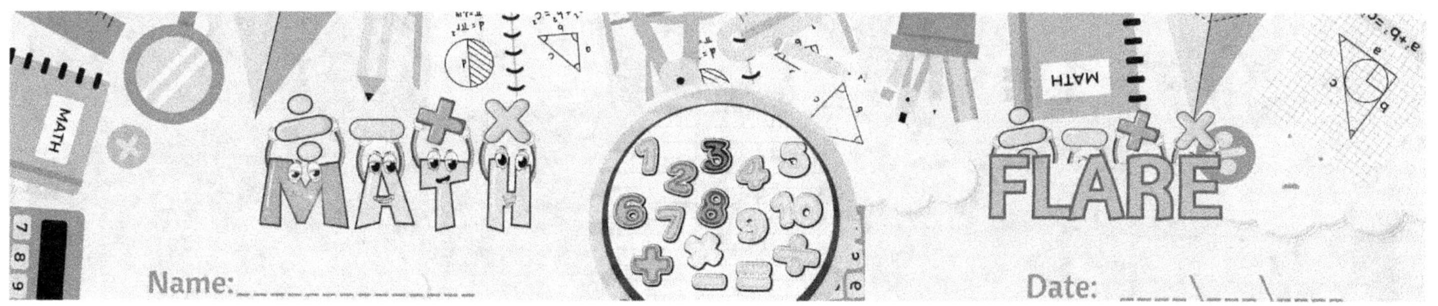

47. $\dfrac{4}{9} = \dfrac{}{54}$

48. $\dfrac{3}{11} = \dfrac{27}{}$

49. $\dfrac{3}{} = \dfrac{6}{24}$

50. $\dfrac{}{10} = \dfrac{81}{90}$

51. $\dfrac{5}{} = \dfrac{30}{36}$

52. $\dfrac{2}{} = \dfrac{20}{40}$

53. $\dfrac{2}{6} = \dfrac{16}{}$

54. $\dfrac{8}{10} = \dfrac{}{80}$

55. $\dfrac{2}{3} = \dfrac{18}{}$

56. $\dfrac{2}{9} = \dfrac{}{63}$

57. $\dfrac{11}{12} = \dfrac{77}{}$

58. $\dfrac{}{2} = \dfrac{8}{16}$

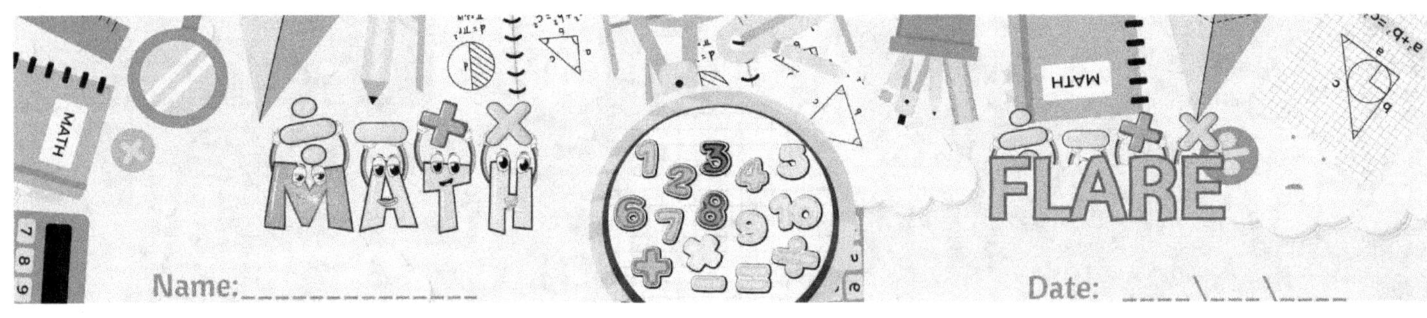

59. $\dfrac{2}{} = \dfrac{8}{16}$

60. $\dfrac{1}{8} = \dfrac{9}{}$

61. $\dfrac{4}{5} = \dfrac{}{25}$

62. $\dfrac{3}{11} = \dfrac{}{44}$

63. $\dfrac{6}{7} = \dfrac{}{35}$

64. $\dfrac{}{10} = \dfrac{24}{30}$

65. $\dfrac{}{11} = \dfrac{10}{22}$

66. $\dfrac{8}{} = \dfrac{56}{63}$

67. $\dfrac{}{8} = \dfrac{8}{32}$

68. $\dfrac{1}{6} = \dfrac{10}{}$

69. $\dfrac{5}{7} = \dfrac{}{42}$

70. $\dfrac{1}{5} = \dfrac{}{50}$

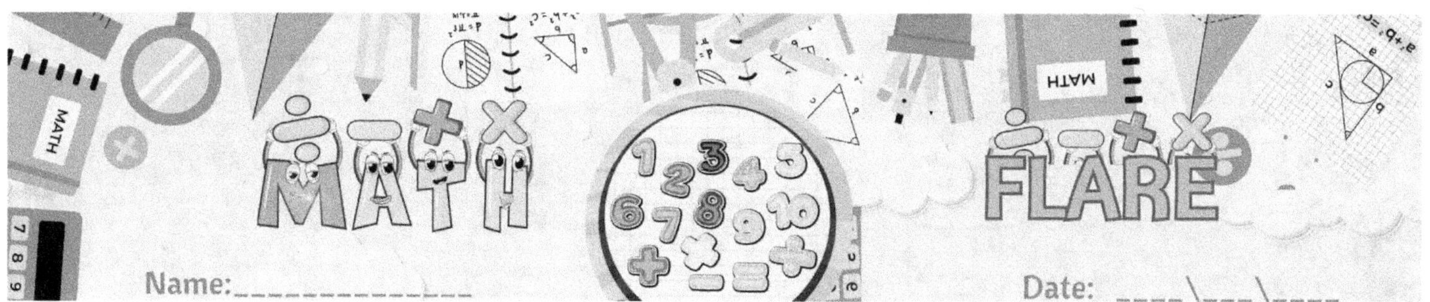

71. $\dfrac{1}{3} = \dfrac{6}{}$

72. $\dfrac{3}{4} = \dfrac{15}{}$

73. $\dfrac{11}{12} = \dfrac{}{60}$

74. $\dfrac{}{9} = \dfrac{18}{27}$

75. $\dfrac{}{12} = \dfrac{15}{36}$

76. $\dfrac{1}{} = \dfrac{10}{100}$

77. $\dfrac{2}{3} = \dfrac{8}{}$

78. $\dfrac{1}{2} = \dfrac{}{18}$

79. $\dfrac{}{4} = \dfrac{2}{8}$

80. $\dfrac{1}{7} = \dfrac{8}{}$

81. $\dfrac{3}{11} = \dfrac{}{66}$

82. $\dfrac{7}{8} = \dfrac{}{32}$

83. $\dfrac{6}{7} = \dfrac{36}{}$

84. $\dfrac{}{10} = \dfrac{10}{20}$

85. $\dfrac{8}{11} = \dfrac{}{55}$

86. $\dfrac{1}{8} = \dfrac{5}{}$

87. $\dfrac{}{6} = \dfrac{32}{48}$

88. $\dfrac{7}{12} = \dfrac{28}{}$

89. $\dfrac{4}{} = \dfrac{28}{35}$

90. $\dfrac{}{3} = \dfrac{20}{30}$

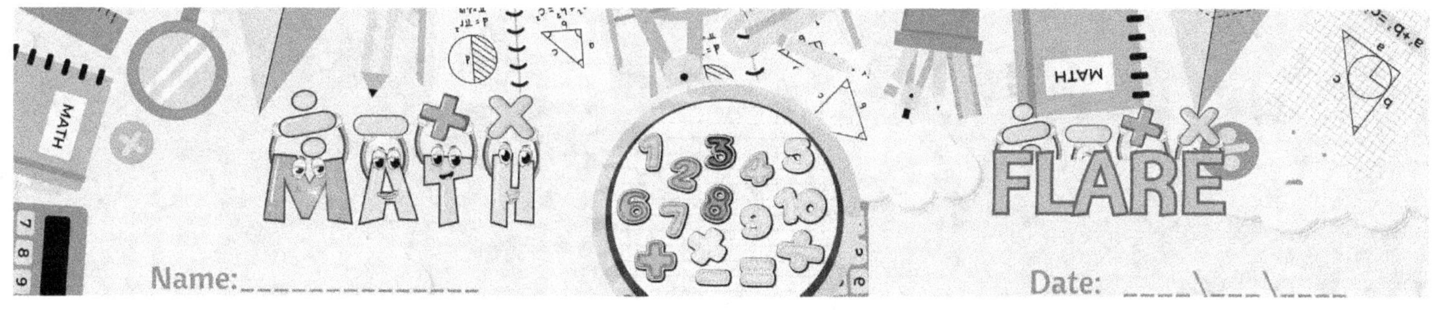

Ratio and Proportion Word Problems

91. If three painters can paint a house in nine days, how many painters are needed to paint the same house in six days?

92. If a recipe calls for four eggs for every 10 cups of flour, how many eggs are needed for 16 cups of flour?

93. If a recipe calls for five eggs for every eight cups of flour, how many eggs are needed for nine cups of flour?

94. A zoo has a ratio of four monkeys to every seven lions. If there are 42 lions in the zoo, how many monkeys are there?

95. A class has a ratio of four girls to every 10 boys. If there are 21 boys, how many girls are there?

96. In a bag of candies, the ratio of chocolate candies to fruit candies is two:nine. If there are 10 fruit candies, how many chocolate candies are there?

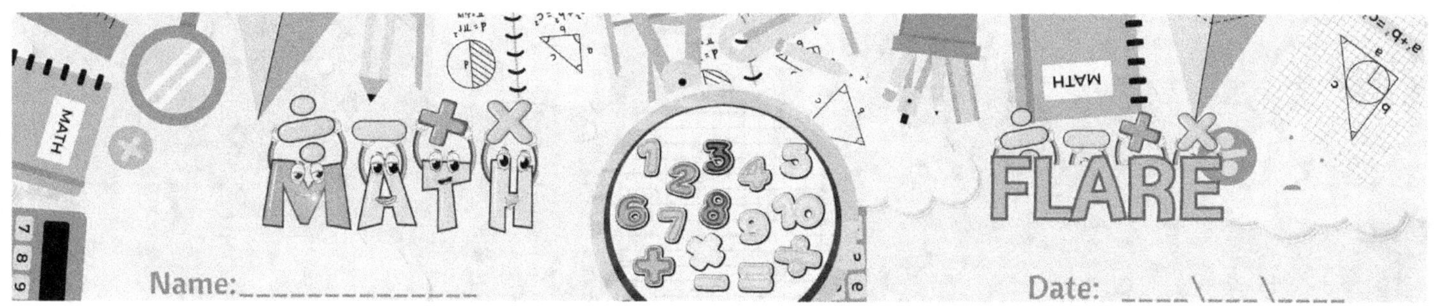

97. If a recipe calls for two teaspoon of salt for every seven cups of flour, how much salt is needed for 11 cups of flour?

98. A train travels 281 miles in five hours. How far can it travel in 11 hours?

99. Addison sells three plates for every six Clipboards. If there are 95 plates, how many Clipboards are there?

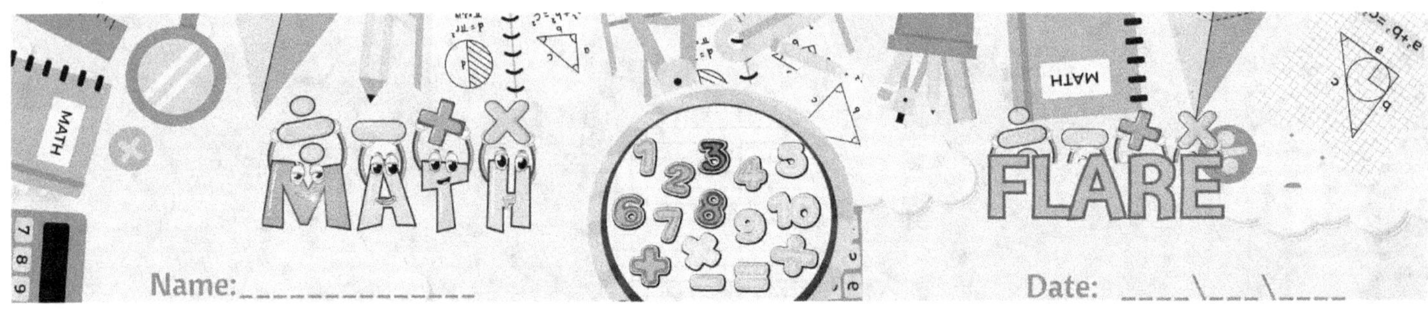

100. In a classroom, the ratio of boys to girls is four:10. If there are 14 girls, how many boys are there?

101. A charity received a donation of $3,376 from a company. If the donation was divided among five charities in the ratio 2:3:4:5:6, how much did the third charity receive?

102. A farmer has a ratio of three sheep to every 10 cows in his pasture. If there are 34 cows in the pasture, how many sheep are there?

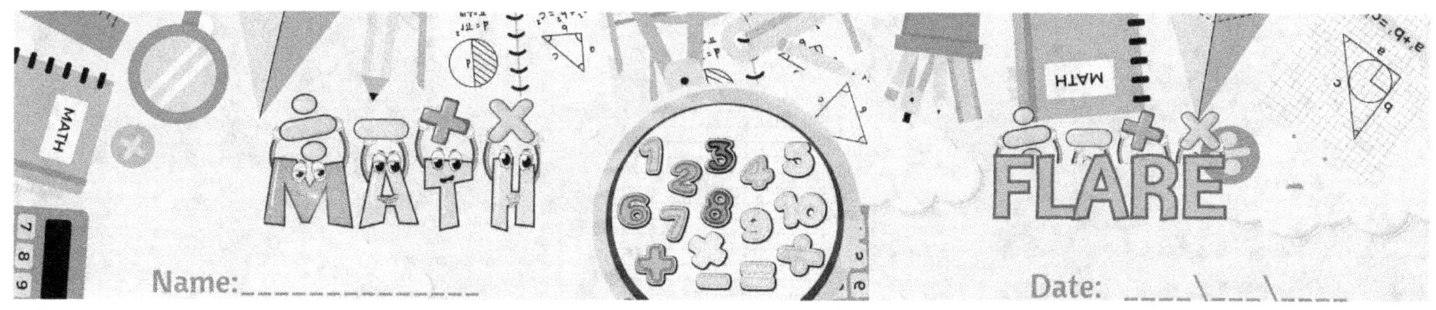

103. If a recipe calls for five cups of sugar for every seven cups of flour, how many cups of sugar are needed for 23 cups of flour?

104. If 10 workers can complete a job in 11 days, how many workers are needed to complete the job in eight days?

105. If it takes three students 19 hours to complete a science project, how many students are needed to finish the project in five hours?

106. A school has a ratio of four teachers for every 20 students. If the school has 135 students, how many teachers are there?

107. A school has a teacher-student ratio of 1:28. If there are 806 students, how many teachers are needed?

108. A bus travels at a speed of 75 miles per hour. How long will it take to travel 164 miles?

109. A grocery store has a ratio of four apples to every six oranges. If there are 37 oranges in the store, how many apples are there?

110. A bike travels at a speed of 30 miles per hour. How long will it take to travel 53 miles?

111. If three workers can build a house in nine hours, how many workers are needed to build the house in six hours?

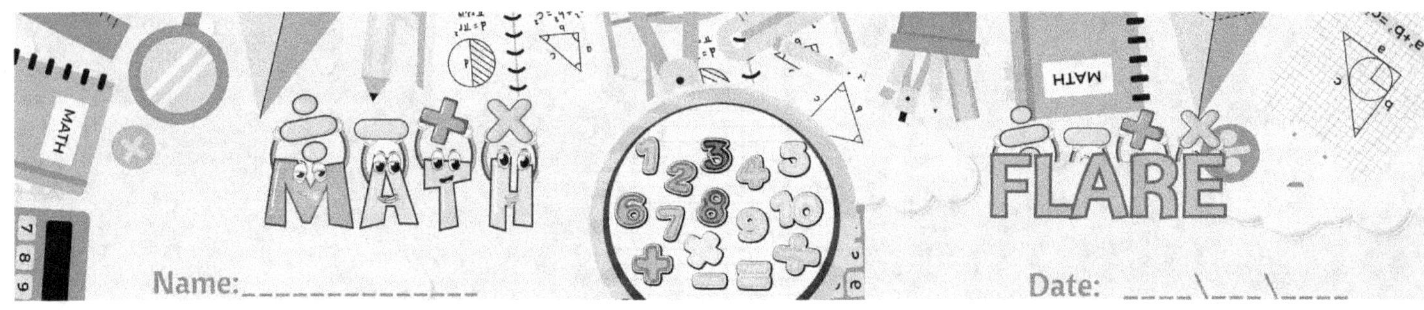

112. A machine can produce 191 units of a product in nine hours. How long will it take to produce 319 units?

113. If a recipe calls for three cups of water for every six cups of rice, how much water is needed for seven cups of rice?

114. A charity received a donation of $1,294 from a company. If the donation was divided among five charities in the ratio 2:3:4:5:6, how much did the fifth charity receive?

Name: _________________   Date: ____________

115. A charity received a donation of $4,006 from a company. If the donation was divided among five charities in the ratio 2:3:4:5:6, how much did the fourth charity receive?

116. If three chefs can bake 100 cakes in 18 hours, how many chefs are needed to bake the same number of cakes in nine hours?

117. If a team of two construction workers can build a road in 12 days, how many workers are required to complete the road in four days?

118. A road is 157 miles long and it takes a car two hour to travel the entire length. What is the speed of the car in miles per hour?

119. A company has a ratio of four female employees to every eight male employees. If there are 21 male employees, how many female employees are there?

120. If eight workers can build a wall in 14 hours, how many workers are needed to build the wall in eight hours?

121. If a map scale is 1 inch to seven miles, how far apart are two cities that are nine inches apart on the map?

122. A train travels 109 miles in two hours. How far can it travel in six hours?

123. A school has a ratio of two female teachers to every six male teachers. If there are 28 male teachers, how many female teachers are there?

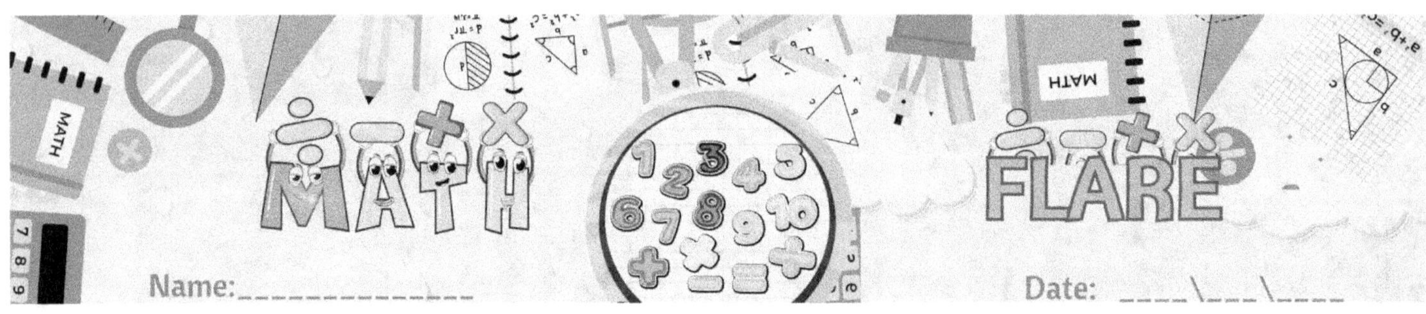

124. If a car travels 173 miles using 13 gallons of gas, how far can it travel using 16 gallons of gas?

125. Emmett drives 185 miles in four hours. How far can he travel in 11 hours?

126. A car can travel 59 miles per gallon of gas. How many gallons of gas are needed to travel 112 miles?

127. If a car travels 474 miles in seven hours, how far can it travel in 10 hours?

128. A recipe calls for four cups of sugar for every 10 cups of flour. If you have 16 cups of flour, how much sugar is needed?

129. A company has a ratio of four managers for every 24 employees. If the company has 173 employees, how many managers are there?

130. A car travels 146 miles in two hours. How far can it travel in seven hours?

131. A bus travels at a speed of 82 miles per hour. How long will it take to travel 176 miles?

132. In a classroom, the ratio of boys to girls is one:seven. If there are 12 girls, how many boys are there?

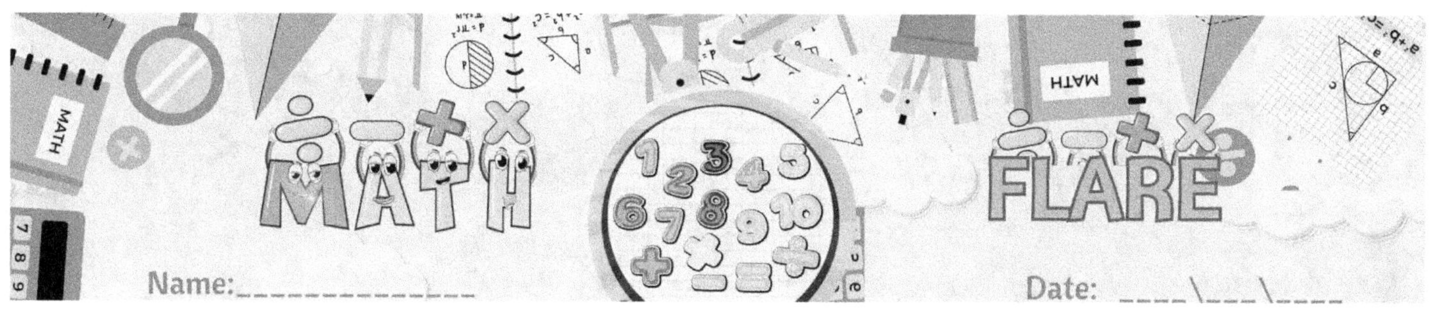

133. If nine workers can complete a job in 12 days, how many workers are needed to complete the job in eight days?

134. If a recipe calls for three cups of sugar for every five cups of flour, how many cups of sugar are needed for 14 cups of flour?

135. A farmer has a ratio of four sheep to every nine cows in his pasture. If there are 38 cows in the pasture, how many sheep are there?

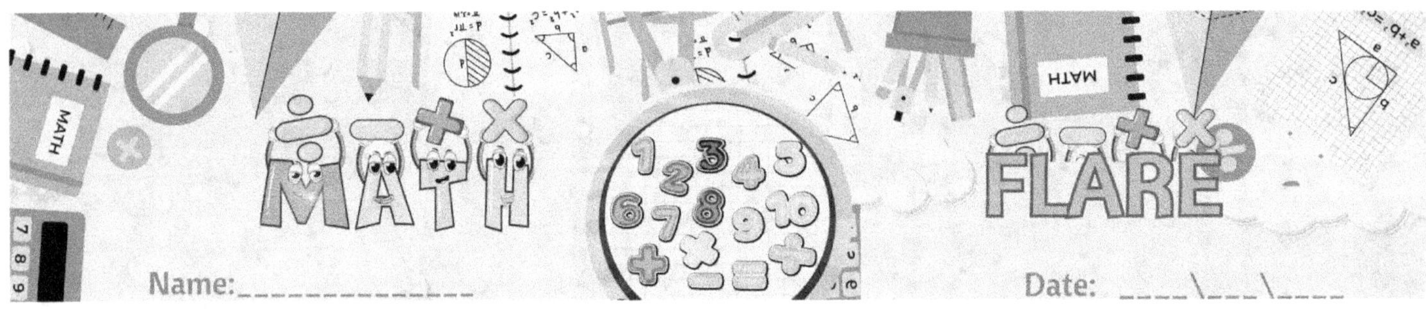

136. If six chefs can bake 100 cakes in 11 hours, how many chefs are needed to bake the same number of cakes in four hours?

137. If 10 painters can paint a house in 14 days, how many painters are needed to paint the same house in eight days?

138. A charity received a donation of $1,191 from a company. If the donation was divided among five charities in the ratio 2:3:4:5:6, how much did the third charity receive?

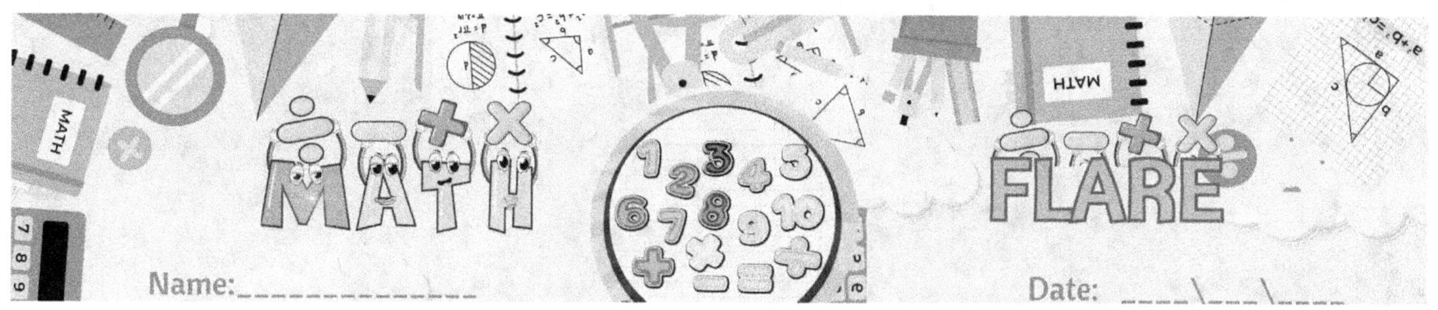

139. If a car travels 629 miles in four hours, how far can it travel in eight hours?

140. A car travels 258 miles in four hours. How far can it travel in six hours?

141. A road is 114 miles long and it takes a car three hour to travel the entire length. What is the speed of the car in miles per hour?

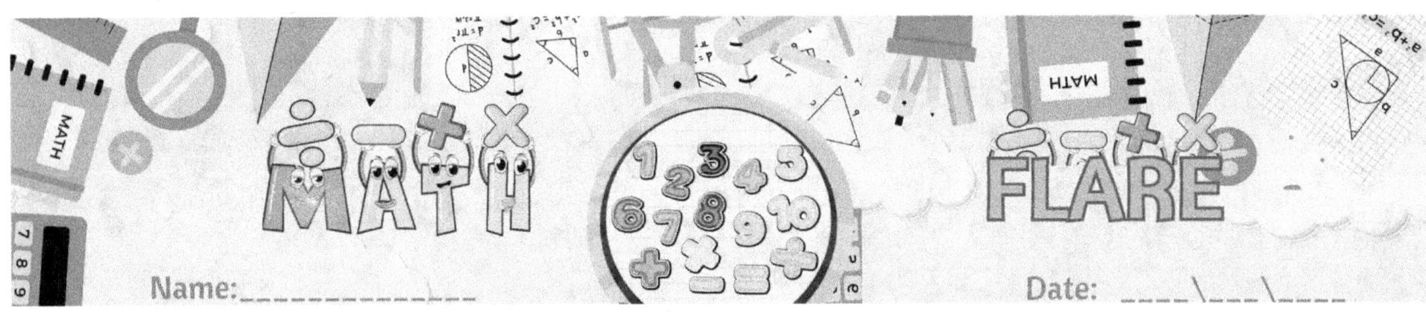

142. A charity received a donation of \$2,364 from a company. If the donation was divided among five charities in the ratio 2:3:4:5:6, how much did the fifth charity receive?

143. If a recipe calls for three cups of water for every five cups of rice, how much water is needed for 10 cups of rice?

144. A school has a ratio of two female teachers to every six male teachers. If there are 20 male teachers, how many female teachers are there?

145. A charity received a donation of $4,967 from a company. If the donation was divided among five charities in the ratio 2:3:4:5:6, how much did the fourth charity receive?

146. A train travels 219 miles in four hours. How far can it travel in 15 hours?

147. A school has a ratio of two teachers for every 25 students. If the school has 112 students, how many teachers are there?

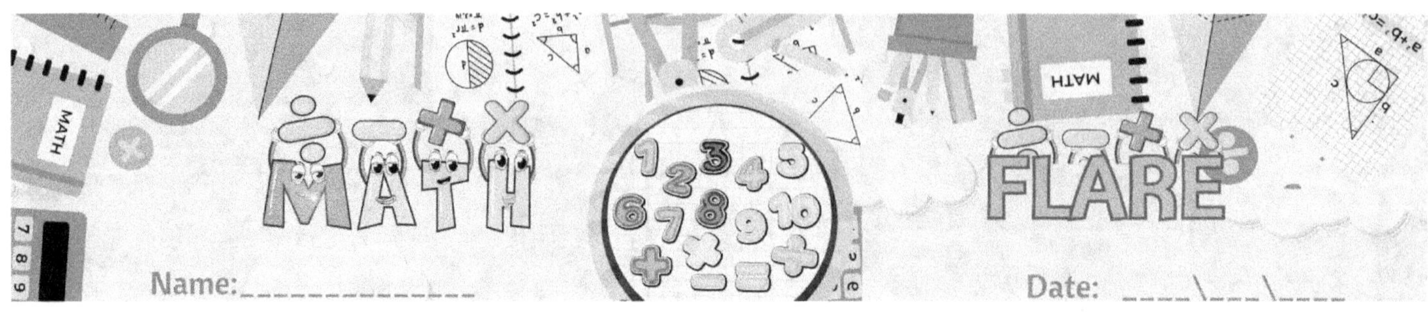

148. If five workers can build a house in 13 hours, how many workers are needed to build the house in nine hours?

149. If a recipe calls for three teaspoon of salt for every five cups of flour, how much salt is needed for 11 cups of flour?

150. If it takes two students 16 hours to complete a science project, how many students are needed to finish the project in 10 hours?

151. If a recipe calls for two eggs for every six cups of flour, how many eggs are needed for 12 cups of flour?

152. A company has a ratio of two managers for every 26 employees. If the company has 149 employees, how many managers are there?

153. A school has a teacher-student ratio of 1:33. If there are 882 students, how many teachers are needed?

154. In a bag of candies, the ratio of chocolate candies to fruit candies is four:10. If there are 12 fruit candies, how many chocolate candies are there?

155. A grocery store has a ratio of four apples to every 10 oranges. If there are 34 oranges in the store, how many apples are there?

156. If a team of eight construction workers can build a road in 14 days, how many workers are required to complete the road in eight days?

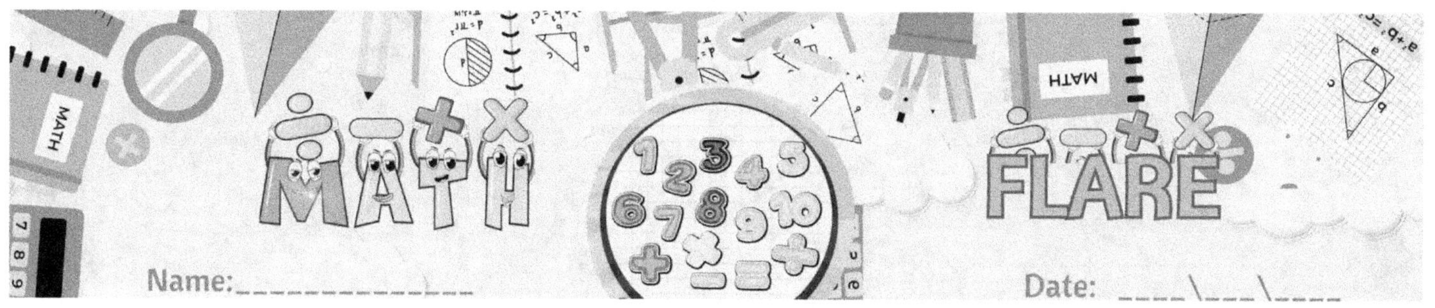

Name:____________________   Date: ______________

157. A train travels 111 miles in four hours. How far can it travel in
seven hours?

158. If a recipe calls for five eggs for every five cups of flour, how
many eggs are needed for 18 cups of flour?

159. If four workers can build a wall in 19 hours, how many workers
are needed to build the wall in 10 hours?

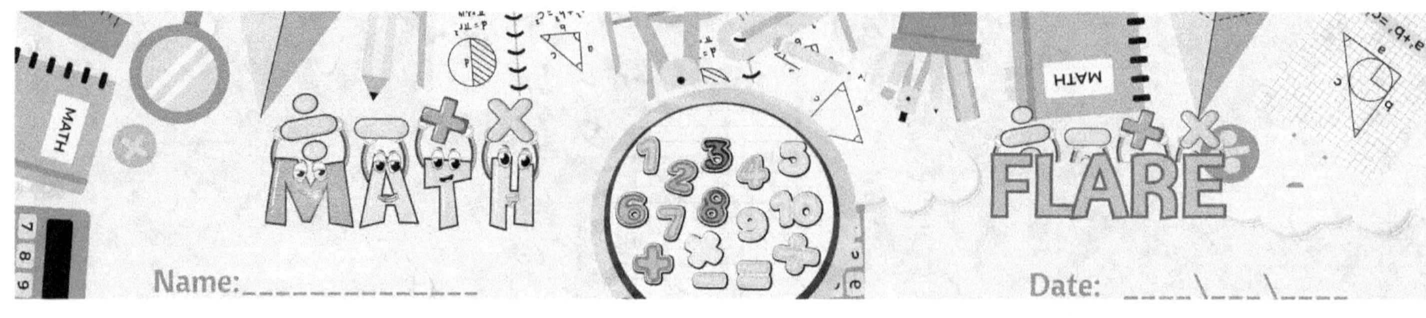

Percentage

Find the percentage of given numbers and percent values.

160. [ ] of 600 = 60

161. 15% of [ ] = 12

162. [ ] of 10 = 7.5

163. 35% of [ ] = 35

164. 30% of [ ] = 90

165. [ ] of 800 = 160

166. [ ] of 900 = 45

167. 25% of [ ] = 225

168. 1% of 700 = [ ]

169. 6% of 100 = [ ]

170. [ ] of 800 = 32

171. 100% of 700 = [ ]

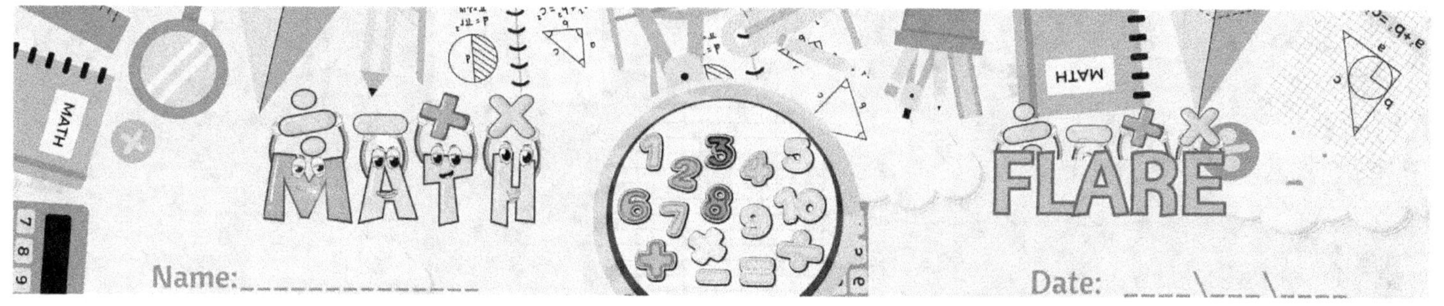

172. 50% of [ ] = 350

173. 40% of [ ] = 160

174. 200% of 70 = [ ]

175. [ ] of 900 = 135

176. [ ] of 500 = 250

177. [ ] of 600 = 54

178. [ ] of 900 = 315

179. 60% of [ ] = 420

180. 5% of [ ] = 20

181. [ ] of 200 = 12

182. [ ] of 800 = 16

183. [ ] of 800 = 64

184. 40% of 200 = ☐

185. ☐ of 300 = 3

186. 300% of ☐ = 30

187. ☐ of 600 = 540

188. ☐ of 200 = 40

189. 10% of 9 = ☐

190. 70% of ☐ = 280

191. 75% of 800 = ☐

192. ☐ of 400 = 320

193. 4% of 100 = ☐

194. ☐ of 300 = 300

195. ☐ of 50 = 15

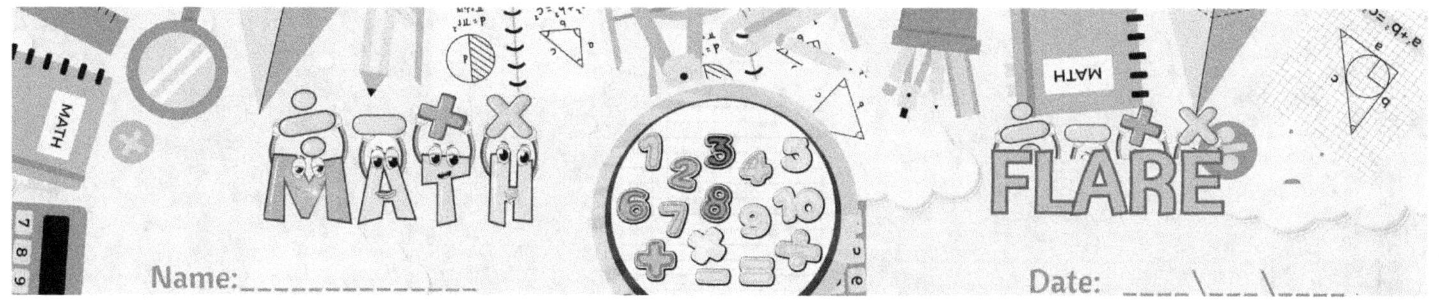

196. 200% of ☐ = 600

197. ☐ of 800 = 24

198. ☐ of 600 = 42

199. ☐ of 600 = 120

200. 10% of ☐ = 90

201. 30% of ☐ = 120

202. 7% of ☐ = 28

203. 90% of 800 = ☐

204. 25% of ☐ = 50

205. 2% of 500 = ☐

206. 4% of 900 = ☐

207. 40% of 500 = ☐

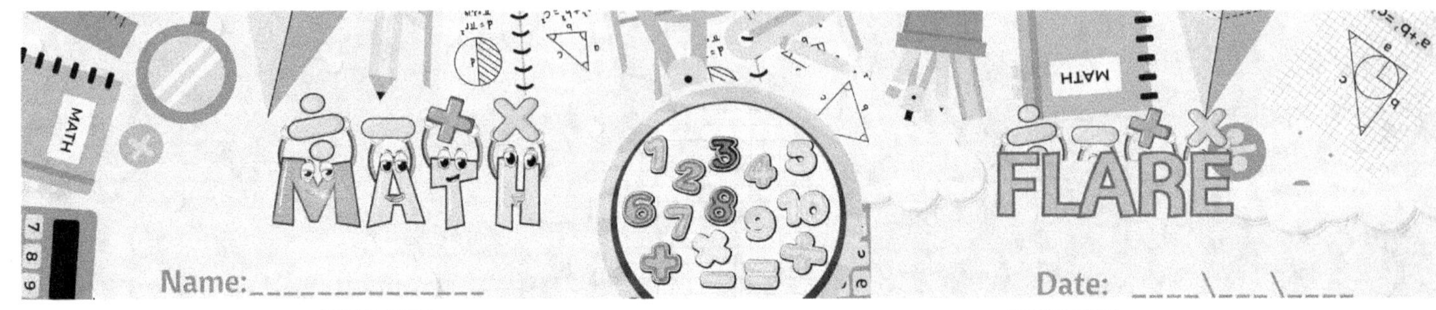

208. 70% of ⬚ = 630

209. 200% of ⬚ = 1400

210. ⬚ of 900 = 540

211. 75% of ⬚ = 300

212. 8% of 200 = ⬚

213. 50% of ⬚ = 50

214. 3% of ⬚ = 27

215. ⬚ of 900 = 720

216. 15% of ⬚ = 105

217. 9% of 300 = ⬚

218. 300% of 900 = ⬚

219. 100% of ⬚ = 400

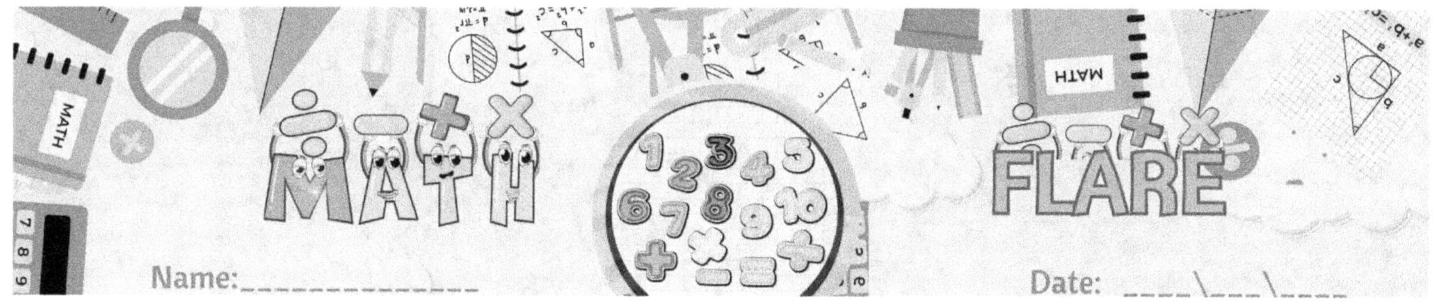

220. 40% of ☐ = 40

221. 90% of 400 = ☐

222. ☐ of 900 = 9

223. 3% of 300 = ☐

224. ☐ of 200 = 200

225. 60% of ☐ = 360

226. 80% of ☐ = 80

227. 10% of 700 = ☐

228. ☐ of 300 = 60

229. 25% of 300 = ☐

230. 50% of 10 = ☐

231. 8% of 900 = ☐

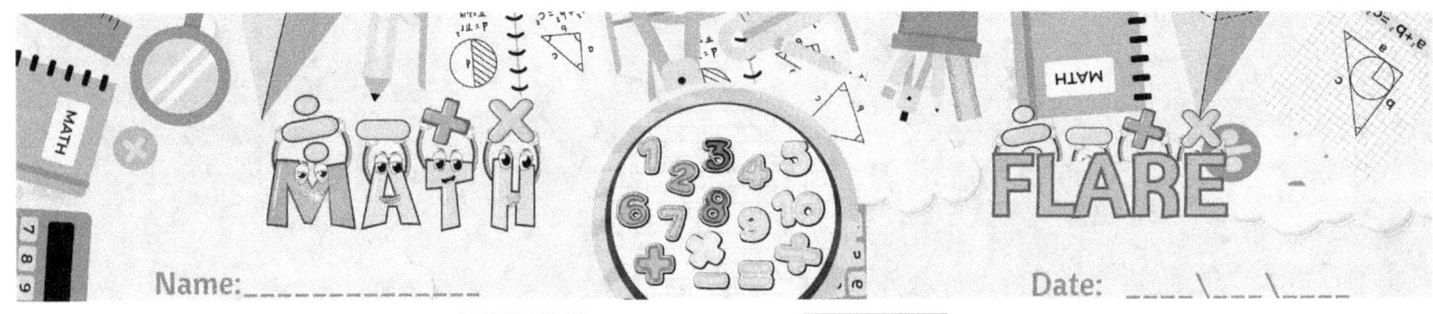

232. 75% of 700 = ☐

233. ☐ of 800 = 56

234. 70% of 600 = ☐

235. ☐ of 400 = 24

236. 15% of ☐ = 30

237. ☐ of 400 = 36

238. 30% of 40 = ☐

239. 7% of 700 = ☐

240. 90% of ☐ = 90

241. 1% of ☐ = 8

242. 100% of 800 = ☐

243. 80% of 200 = ☐

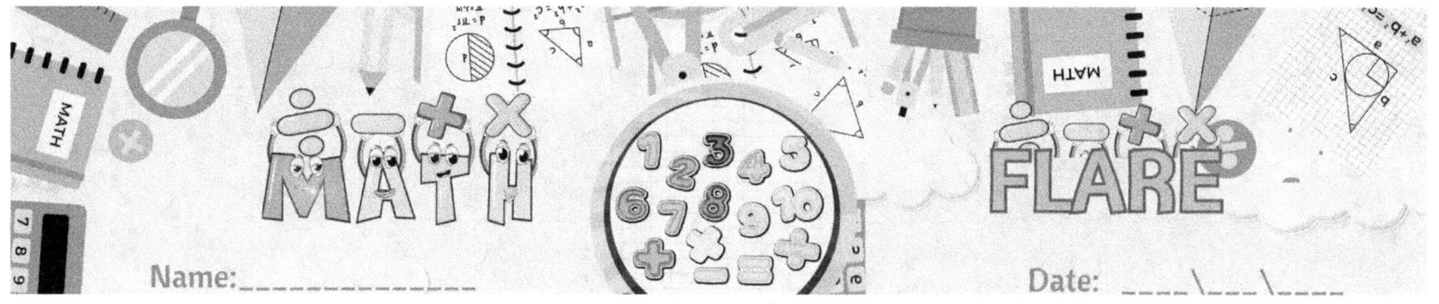

244. 40% of 2 = [ ]

245. [ ] of 300 = 225

246. 70% of 200 = [ ]

247. 20% of 900 = [ ]

248. [ ] of 300 = 150

249. [ ] of 500 = 40

250. 30% of [ ] = 2.4

251. 5% of [ ] = 30

252. [ ] of 700 = 14

253. 4% of 500 = [ ]

254. 300% of [ ] = 2400

255. 200% of 100 = [ ]

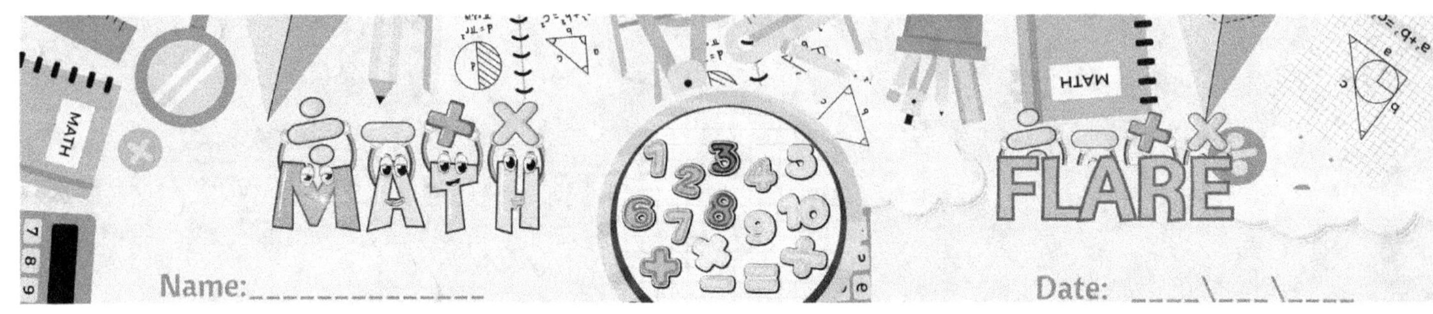

256. [ ] of 200 = 100

257. 30% of 900 = [ ]

258. 80% of 700 = [ ]

259. 300% of 500 = [ ]

260. [ ] of 61 = 21.594

261. [ ] of 97 = 11.349

262. 13.4% of [ ] = 112.694

263. 36.6% of 310 = [ ]

264. 1.3% of [ ] = 9.75

265. [ ] of 5 = 0.155

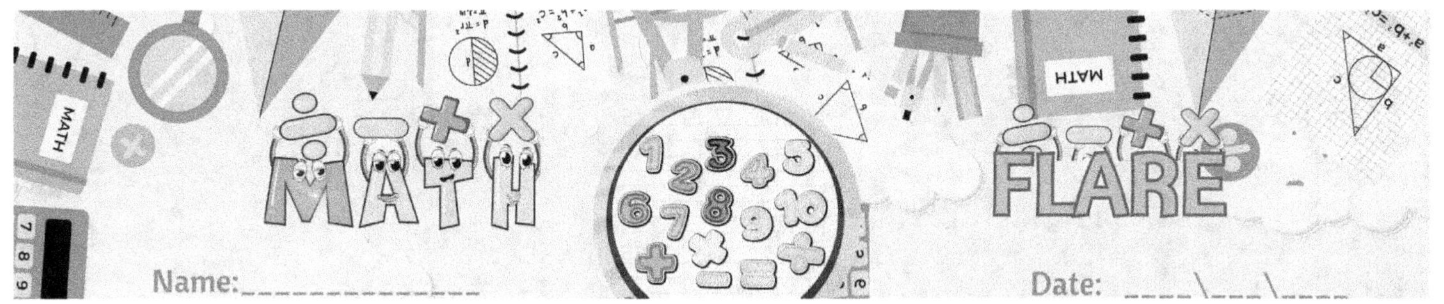

266. 3.3% of 22 = [ ]

267. [ ] of 784 = 7.056

268. 3.0% of 11 = [ ]

269. 4.2% of [ ] = 0.714

270. 40.5% of 82 = [ ]

271. 2.7% of [ ] = 1.809

272. 0.7% of [ ] = 0.035

273. 0.2% of 4 = [ ]

274. 0.7% of [ ] = 0.014

275. [ ] of 5 = 1.47

276. 8.8% of 94 = ☐

277. ☐ of 6 = 1.488

278. 3.1% of 434 = ☐

279. 41.9% of 69 = ☐

280. ☐ of 3 = 0.015

281. 2.7% of ☐ = 26.325

282. 0.5% of 85 = ☐

283. 17.0% of ☐ = 11.39

284. 0.2% of 5 = ☐

285. 2.2% of ☐ = 0.132

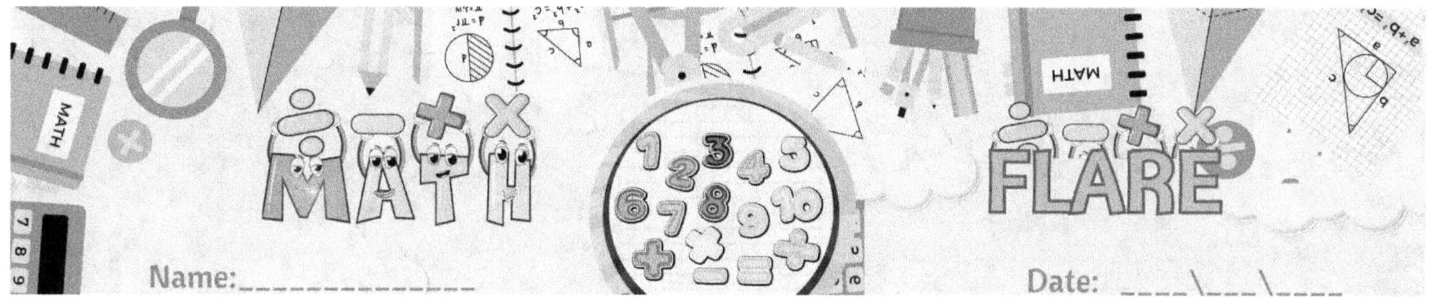

286. 7.8% of 83 = ☐

287. 0.5% of 7 = ☐

288. ☐ of 461 = 13.369

289. 0.3% of 540 = ☐

290. ☐ of 8 = 1.568

291. 1.6% of ☐ = 0.848

292. ☐ of 495 = 175.23

293. 11.7% of ☐ = 0.468

294. 13.4% of ☐ = 38.458

295. 36.6% of 77 = ☐

Name:______________________   Date: _______________

296. 1.3% of 184 = [____]

297. [____] of 597 = 18.507

298. [____] of 5 = 0.165

299. [____] of 5 = 0.045

300. 3.0% of 6 = [____]

301. 4.2% of [____] = 30.45

302. 40.5% of 8 = [____]

303. 2.7% of 37 = [____]

304. 0.7% of [____] = 0.168

305. [____] of 231 = 0.462

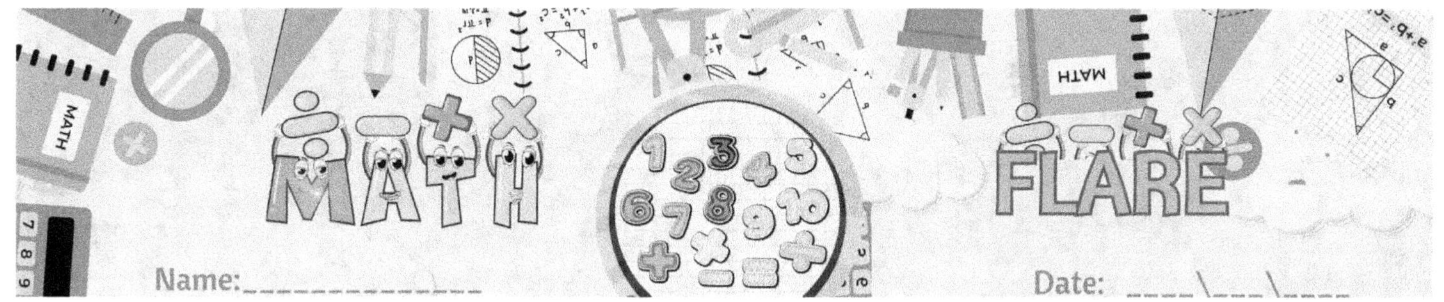

306. _______ of 844 = 5.908   307. 29.4% of _______ = 2.646

308. 8.8% of 16 = _______   309. 24.8% of 921 = _______

310. 3.1% of 94 = _______   311. 41.9% of _______ = 418.162

312. 0.5% of _______ = 0.025   313. _______ of 387 = 10.449

314. _______ of 544 = 2.72   315. 17.0% of _______ = 53.04

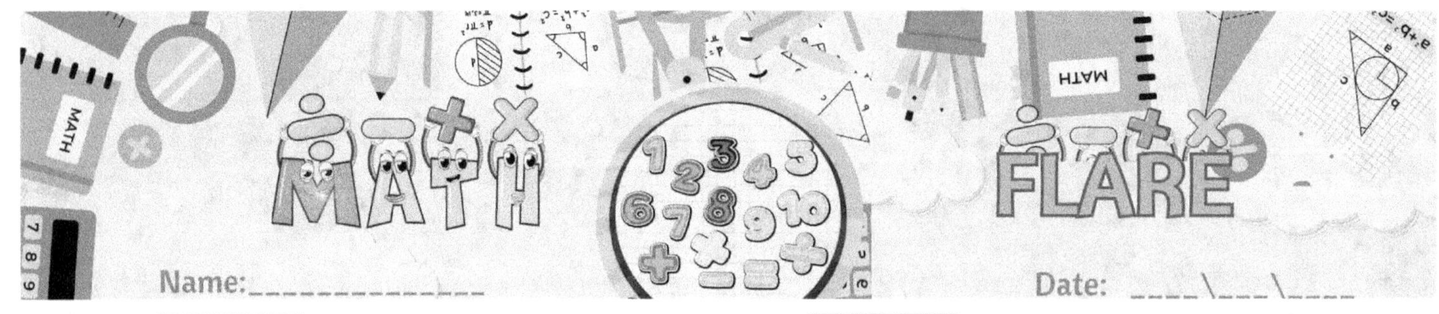

316. [   ] of 3 = 0.006

317. [   ] of 61 = 0.427

318. [   ] of 793 = 17.446

319. 7.8% of 1 = [   ]

320. [   ] of 724 = 3.62

321. 2.9% of 703 = [   ]

322. 0.3% of 38 = [   ]

323. [   ] of 942 = 184.632

324. 1.6% of [   ] = 15.936

325. [   ] of 1 = 0.354

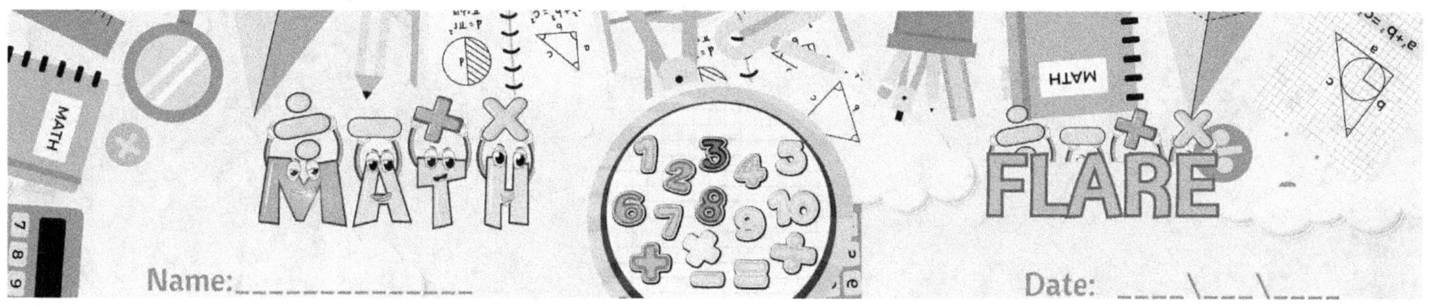

326. 11.7% of [ ] = 4.095

327. 13.4% of 260 = [ ]

328. [ ] of 928 = 339.648

329. 1.3% of 83 = [ ]

330. 3.1% of [ ] = 9.021

331. 0.9% of 50 = [ ]

332. [ ] of 679 = 20.37

333. 4.2% of 58 = [ ]

334. 40.5% of 7 = [ ]

335. 2.7% of [ ] = 25.164

336. 0.7% of 9 = ⬚

337. 0.2% of 1 = ⬚

338. 0.7% of 80 = ⬚

339. 29.4% of ⬚ = 28.812

340. ⬚ of 8 = 0.704

341. 24.8% of ⬚ = 16.368

342. 3.1% of 928 = ⬚

343. 41.9% of ⬚ = 11.313

344. 0.5% of 986 = ⬚

345. 2.7% of ⬚ = 0.108

Word Problems: Percent

346. Willow bought a camera for $25.00. If she paid an additional 52% for sales tax, how much in total did she pay for the camera?

347. In a class of 8 students, 25% are boys. How many are boys?

348. What is 25% of 8?

349. A teacher gave a math test with 44 questions. If a student got 25% questions correct, how many questions were correct?

350. In a class of 16 students, 25% are girls. How many are girls?

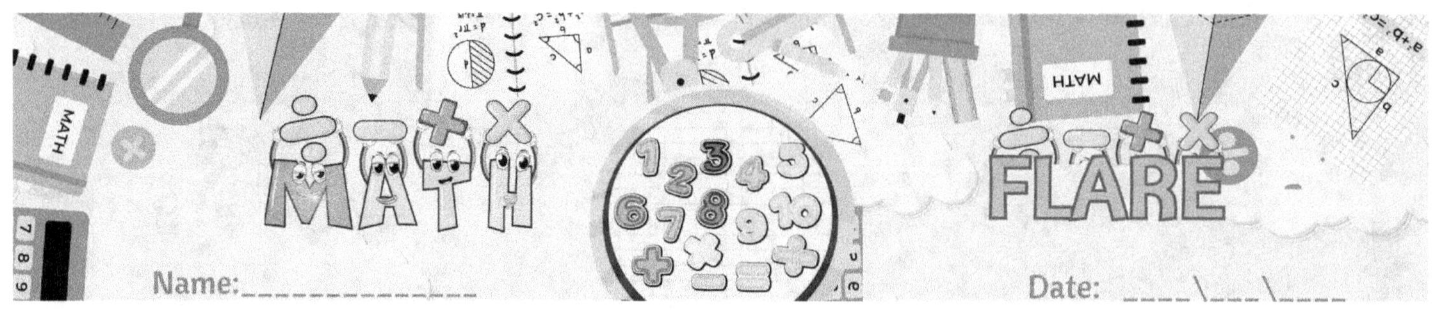

351. A person wants to make a 25% tip on a $8.00 meal. How much should the tip be?

352. Kai earned $52.00 for a week's work. If he paid 25% of it in taxes how much did he pay in taxes?

353. A restaurant makes a pizza that is 48 inches in diameter. If they want to increase the size of the pizza by 25%, what will be the new diameter?

354. A school has 24 students. If 25% of them play baseball, how many students play baseball?

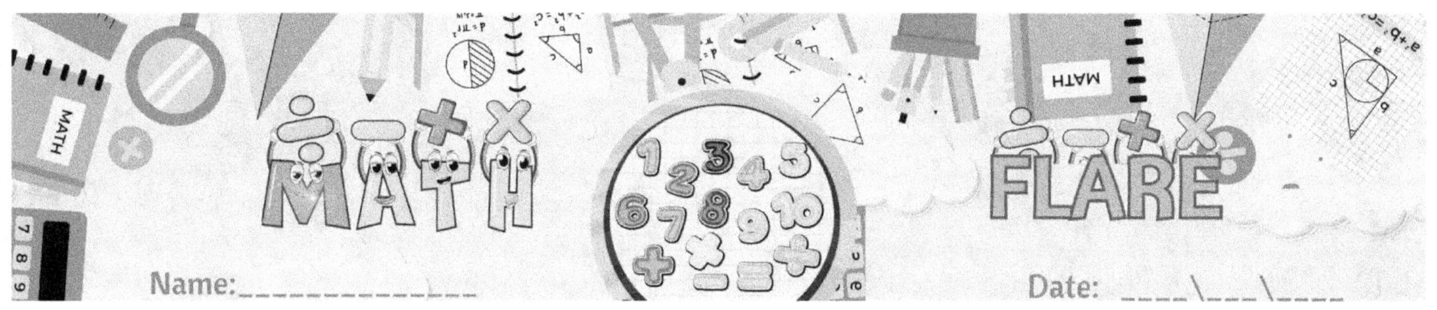

355. A store is having a sale where everything is 81% off. The flosses originally priced at $100.00 is now on sale. How much is the new price of flosses now?

356. Maverick had 4 rocks. He gave away 25% of them. How many did he have left?

357. A store increases the prices of all items by 81%. If the candies originally costs $100.00, what is the sale price?

358. In a survey of 4 people, 25% said they preferred android OS. How many people preferred android OS?

359. Hannah had a collection of 75 baseball cards. She gave away 52% of them. How many did she have left?

360. Leah bought perfumes for $50.00. If she paid an additional 4% for sales tax, how much in total did she pay for the perfumes?

361. A company wants to increase its revenue by 12%. If its current revenue is $75.00 million, what should be its new revenue?

362. A classroom has 16 students, of which 25% are girls. How many boys are in the classroom?

363. If the number 75 is decreased by 4%, what is the value of the new number?

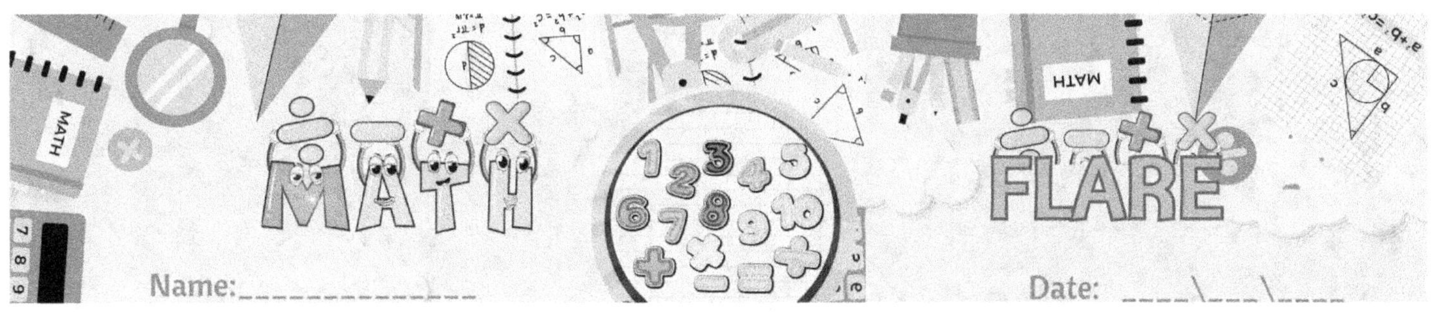

364. Lila bought some folders for $52.00. If she paid an additional 25% for sales tax, how much in total did she pay for the folders?

365. A store offers a 4% discount on all items. If Jade buys trees originally priced at $75.00, how much money did she save?

366. If the number 25 is increased by 4%, what is the value of the new number?

367. A car dealership sold 50 cars last month. If the sales increased by 12% this month, how many cars did they sell this month?

368. A store has 68 cakes. If 25% of them are sold at the end of the day, how many cakes are sold?

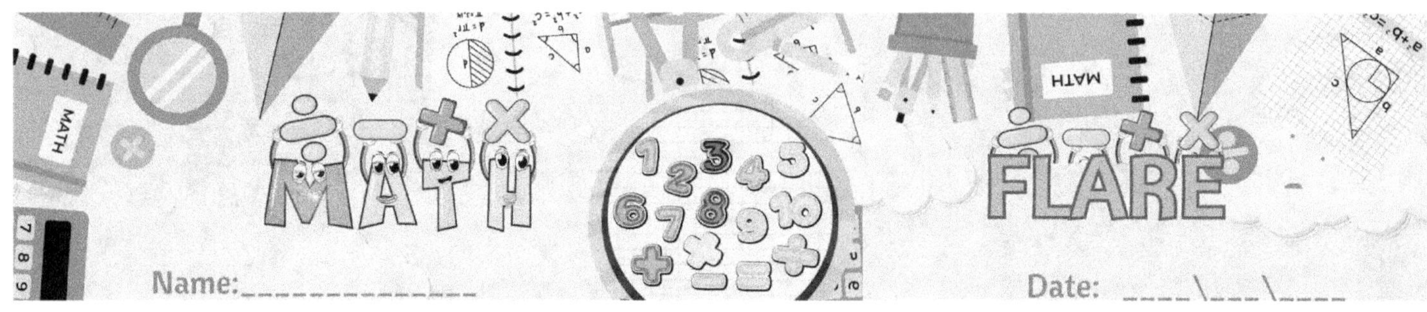

369. In a basket of 50 balls, 4% are red balls . How many are red balls?

370. In a class of 25 students, 72% of them are in the Math Club. How many students are in the Math Club?

371. Kai's monthly sales of flowers was $96.00. If he earned 25% of profit, what was his profit?

372. William bought a bicycle that cost $75.00 when it was new. If he eventually sold it for 4% of the original cost, how much was it sold for?

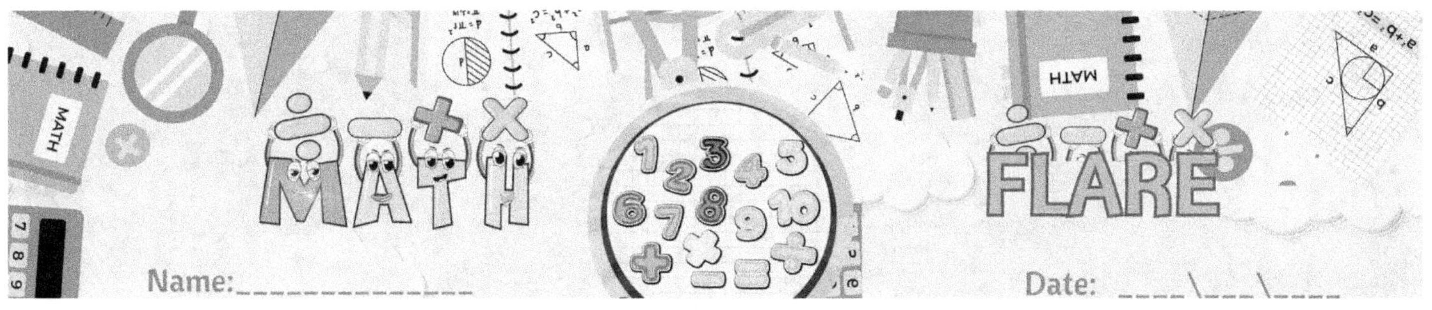

373. Natalia bought a bag for $75.00. If she paid an additional 36% for sales tax, how much in total did she pay for the bag?

374. Eva bought a pizza for $25.00. If she paid an additional 72% for sales tax, how much in total did she pay for the pizza?

375. A school has 52 students. If 25% of them play football, how many students play football?

376. In a survey of 50 people, 72% said they prefer cats over dogs. How many people prefer cats?

377. A store offers 4% discount on all products. If the sale price of shoes was 25, what was the original price?

378. Owen buys bananas for $84.00 to sell them in market. If he wants to earn 25% profit. What must be the selling price of bananas?

379. Madison bought a shoes for $4.00. If she paid an additional 25% for sales tax, how much in total did she pay for the shoes?

380. A school has a total of 50 teachers. If 4% of them are men, how many male teachers are there?

381. A school has 40 students. If 5% of them play tennis, how many students play tennis?

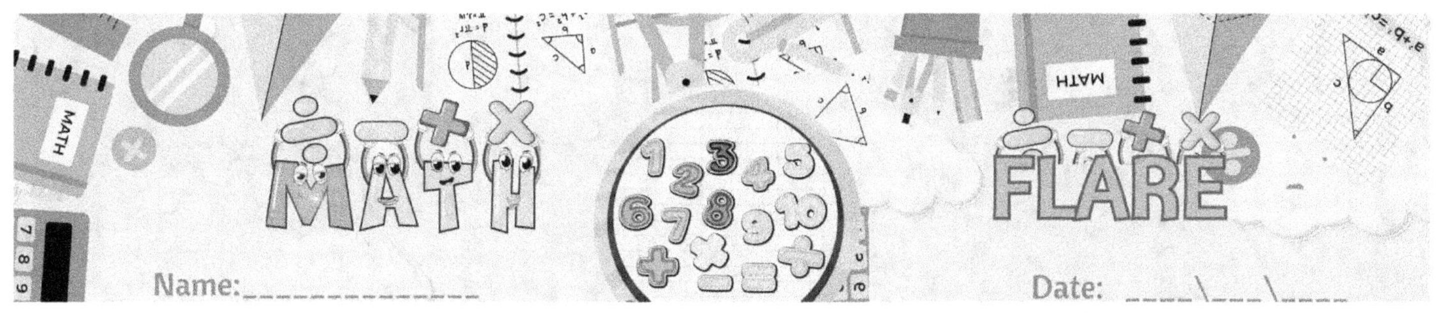

382. Peyton bought a book for $80.00. If she paid an additional 5% for sales tax, how much in total did she pay for the book?

383. A store offers 36% discount on all products. If the original price of bags was 50, what is the sales price?

384. A school has a total of 92 teachers. If 25% of them are men, how many female teachers are there?

385. In a school of 100 students, 7% of them take the bus to school. How many students take the bus?

386. In a class of 25 students, 4% are girls. How many are girls?

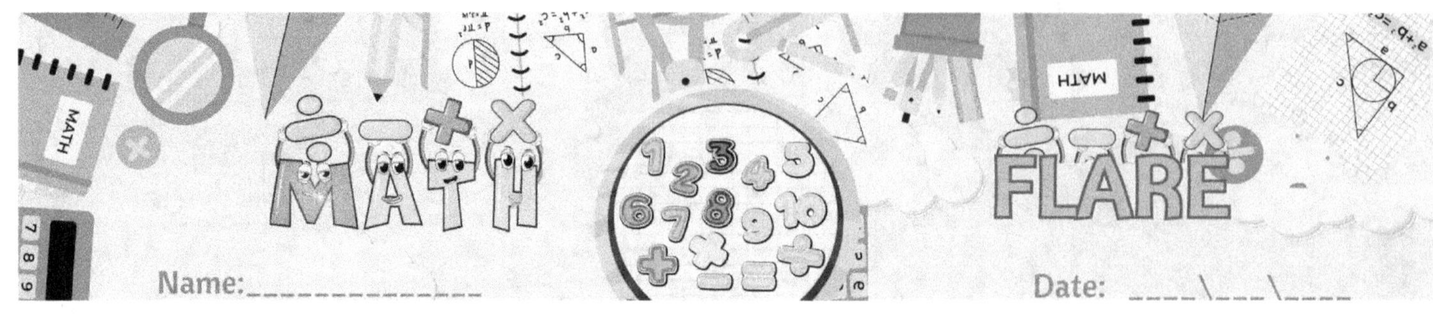

387. A store has 75 erasers. If 52% of them are sold at the end of the day, how many erasers are sold?

388. A classroom has 20 students, of which 5% are girls. How many boys are in the classroom?

389. If the number 8 is increased by 25%, what is the value of the new number?

390. Olivia bought a shoes for $8.00. If she paid an additional 25% for sales tax, how much in total did she pay for the shoes?

391. A school has 50 students. If 4% of them play baseball, how many students play baseball?

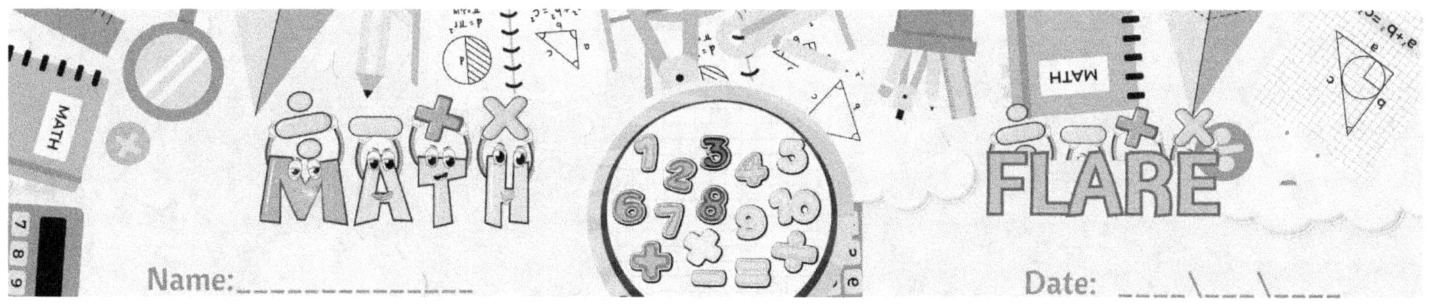

392. A person wants to make a 25% tip on a $56.00 meal. How much should the tip be?

393. A school has a total of 50 teachers. If 94% of them are men, how many female teachers are there?

394. In a survey of 96 people, 25% said they preferred android OS. How many people preferred android OS?

395. A store is having a sale where everything is 4% off. The pants originally priced at $25.00 is now on sale. How much is the new price of pants now?

ANSWERS

Page 1: Proportional Relationship

1. 10	2. 20	3. 2	4. 32	5. 21	6. 16	7. 20
8. 8	9. 48	10. 1	11. 9	12. 60	13. 55	14. 49
15. 45	16. 1	17. 18	18. 3	19. 5	20. 4	21. 18
22. 4	23. 10	24. 4	25. 100	26. 12	27. 2	28. 7
29. 16	30. 8	31. 1	32. 10	33. 3	34. 9	35. 6
36. 8	37. 6	38. 84	39. 9	40. 20	41. 9	42. 18
43. 11	44. 16	45. 70	46. 35	47. 24	48. 99	49. 12
50. 9	51. 6	52. 4	53. 48	54. 64	55. 27	56. 14
57. 84	58. 1	59. 4	60. 72	61. 20	62. 12	63. 30
64. 8	65. 5	66. 9	67. 2	68. 60	69. 30	70. 10
71. 18	72. 20	73. 55	74. 6	75. 5	76. 10	77. 12
78. 9	79. 1	80. 56	81. 18	82. 28	83. 42	84. 5
85. 40	86. 40	87. 4	88. 48	89. 5	90. 2	

Page 9: Ratio and Proportion Word Problems

91. 4.5	92. 6.4	93. 5.62	94. 24	95. 8.4
96. 2.22	97. 3.14	98. 618.2	99. 190	100. 5.6
101. 675.2	102. 10.2	103. 16.43	104. 13.75	105. 11.4
106. 27	107. 28.79	108. 2.19	109. 24.67	110. 1.77
111. 4.5	112. 15.03	113. 3.5	114. 388.2	115. 1,001.5

116. 6	117. 6	118. 78.5	119. 10.5	120. 14
121. 63	122. 327	123. 9.33	124. 212.92	125. 508.75
126. 1.90	127. 677.14	128. 6.4	129. 28.83	130. 511
131. 2.15	132. 1.71	133. 13.5	134. 8.4	135. 16.89
136. 16.5	137. 17.5	138. 238.2	139. 1,258	140. 387
141. 38	142. 709.2	143. 6	144. 6.67	145. 1,241.75
146. 821.25	147. 8.96	148. 7.22	149. 6.6	150. 3.2
151. 4	152. 11.46	153. 26.73	154. 4.8	155. 13.6
156. 14	157. 194.25	158. 18	159. 7.6	

Page 32: Percentage

160. 10%	161. 80	162. 75%	163. 100	164. 300
165. 20%	166. 5%	167. 900	168. 7	169. 6
170. 4%	171. 700	172. 700	173. 400	174. 140
175. 15%	176. 50%	177. 9%	178. 35%	179. 700
180. 400	181. 6%	182. 2%	183. 8%	184. 80
185. 1%	186. 10	187. 90%	188. 20%	189. 0.9
190. 400	191. 600	192. 80%	193. 4	194. 100%
195. 30%	196. 300	197. 3%	198. 7%	199. 20%
200. 900	201. 400	202. 400	203. 720	204. 200
205. 10	206. 36	207. 200	208. 900	209. 700
210. 60%	211. 400	212. 16	213. 100	214. 900

215. 80% 216. 700 217. 27 218. 2700 219. 400

220. 100 221. 360 222. 1% 223. 9 224. 100%

225. 600 226. 100 227. 70 228. 20% 229. 75

230. 5 231. 72 232. 525 233. 7% 234. 420

235. 6% 236. 200 237. 9% 238. 12 239. 49

240. 100 241. 800 242. 800 243. 160 244. 0.8

245. 75% 246. 140 247. 180 248. 50% 249. 8%

250. 8 251. 600 252. 2% 253. 20 254. 800

255. 200 256. 50% 257. 270 258. 560 259. 1500

Page 40: Percent

260. 35.4% 261. 11.7% 262. 841 263. 113.46

264. 750 265. 3.1% 266. 0.726 267. 0.9%

268. 0.33 269. 17 270. 33.21 271. 67

272. 5 273. 0.008 274. 2 275. 29.4%

276. 8.272 277. 24.8% 278. 13.454 279. 28.911

280. 0.5% 281. 975 282. 0.425 283. 67

284. 0.01 285. 6 286. 6.474 287. 0.035

288. 2.9% 289. 1.62 290. 19.6% 291. 53

292. 35.4% 293. 4 294. 287 295. 28.182

296. 2.392 297. 3.1% 298. 3.3% 299. 0.9%

300. 0.18 301. 725 302. 3.24 303. 0.999

304. 24

305. 0.2%

306. 0.7%

307. 9

308. 1.408

309. 228.408

310. 2.914

311. 998

312. 5

313. 2.7%

314. 0.5%

315. 312

316. 0.2%

317. 0.7%

318. 2.2%

319. 0.078

320. 0.5%

321. 20.387

322. 0.114

323. 19.6%

324. 996

325. 35.4%

326. 35

327. 34.84

328. 36.6%

329. 1.079

330. 291

331. 0.45

332. 3.0%

333. 2.436

334. 2.835

335. 932

336. 0.063

337. 0.002

338. 0.56

339. 98

340. 8.8%

341. 66

342. 28.768

343. 27

344. 4.93

345. 4

Page 49: Word Problems: Percent

346. $38.00

347. 2

348. 2

349. 11

350. 4

351. $2.00

352. $13.00

353. 60

354. 6

355. $19.00

356. 3

357. $181.00

358. 1

359. 36

360. $52.00

361. $84.00

362. 12

363. 72

364. $65.00

365. $3.00

366. 24

367. 56

368. 17

369. 2

370. 18

371. $24.00

372. $3.00

373. $102.00

374. $43.00

375. 13

376. 36

377. 26

378. $105.00

379. $5.00

380. 2

381. 2

382. $84.00

383. 32

384. 69

385. 7

386. 1

387. 39

388. 19

389. 6

390. $10.00

391. 2

392. $14.00

393. 3

394. 24

395. $24.00